A Milestone Journey: Memories and Lessons Throughout the Years

Christian Tomko

A MILESTONE JOURNEY:

Memories and Lessons
Throughout the Years

By

CHRISTIAN TOMKO

A MILESTONE JOURNEY:
Memories and Lessons Throughout the Years
By Christian Tomko

First Edition: July 14, 2022

Printed in the United States of America

ISBN: 9798837856631

Cover design by Catherine Hughes
Cover photo taken by Catherine Hughes
Editing by Catherine Hughes and Betty C. Tomko
Foreword by Catherine Hughes

DISCLAIMER AND LEGAL NOTICES

TABLE OF CONTENTS

FOREWORD

Afters a challenging pregnancy -- and many false starts with my labor -- I gave birth to my wonderful boy, Christian Tyler Tomko, by Cesarean section on January 12, 1998. I was surrounded by my parents and close friends. I was facing a new chapter of my life as a single mother – of course, I was scared. I was unsure if I would be able to be the parent I wanted to be because I was so young (nineteen to be exact). However, I kept the faith that we were meant for a greater purpose. Almost twenty-five years later, I wish that I could go back in time and reassure my younger self that everything would be OK, and trust the Universe's divine timing.

Christian was diagnosed with a form of autism spectrum disorder when he was three years old. There's a story behind the incident that led to that discovery, and many other facets of our journey in my bestselling book *Imprisoned No More: A Mother and Son Embrace Autism and Journey to Freedom.* On my father's (Christian's beloved Grandpa) deathbed, I promised that our story would be told and that I would embrace my childhood dream of becoming a writer. How overjoyed Dad must be in his heavenly eternal life watching his grandson follow in those footsteps!

Something important to note about both my book and, more importantly, the one you are about to read, is that neither one will provide a roadmap about diagnostic criteria, what therapy approach works best, or how to obtain services. There are plenty of other amazing books you can access that serve that purpose quite well.

A Milestone Journey: Memories and Lessons Throughout the Years provides a historical account from the brilliant mind of an autistic man in his mid-twenties who once was non-speaking. Now, to be honest, you will not find many mentions of autism at all in this book! That is because Christian has created a biography that focuses on special moments, favorite pastimes, people that have meant the most to him, and reflections on lessons learned. He's telling *his story, his way*. Who could ask for anything more?

It is an honor for me to share that this book marks the twentieth project that I have been a part of, and I am deeply humbled that my son asked my mother and I to contribute to it.

At the end of *Imprisoned No More*, I provided this as my final dedication:

Saving the best for last, thank you to my only son Christian Tyler Tomko. Our (now twenty-four) year journey together, filled with both challenges and triumphs, has given me great purpose, endless joy, and tremendous pride beyond measure. You are a legend, and you do not even realize it. Your humility is profound.

My son, it is ultimately *you* who has taught *me*.

Without further adieu, it is my honor to introduce you to the one, the only, Christian Tomko.

– Catherine Hughes

About Catherine Hughes

Photo Credit: Jackie Carlantonio

Hailing from a small town southeast of Pittsburgh, Pennsylvania, dubbed "the most boring town in Pennsylvania," Catherine Hughes is the daughter of two English professors. She is a passionate advocate, innovative storyteller, and community strategist.

Catherine is an international best-selling author and/or editor of nearly twenty books. Her long-awaited memoir, Imprisoned No More: A Mother and

Son Embrace Autism and Journey to Freedom released in August 2020. She presented her father's poetry (Seeking Utopia: The Art, Poems, and Passages of John J. Tomko) on what would have been his 77th birthday (1/16/21). The release of both of these books (and all of her other projects) fulfill the promise she made to her father in his final days.

Catherine has managed a blog and social media platforms as The Caffeinated Advocate since 2018. In August 2020, Catherine not only released her memoir, but also founded The Caffeinated Advocate, LLC. She is the Chief Inspirational Officer (CIO), and offers a wide array of services as an author, editor, coach, consultant, speaker, and trainer. She is a Certified Master Life Coach, with certifications endorsed by Transformation Academy of Clearwater, Florida. She partners with Grace & Hope Consulting, LLC as a coach and as their Editor-in-Chief, and with Sunnie Vibes Studio Yoga & Wellness in her hometown to offer life coaching supports and journaling workshops.

For two decades, she has provided comprehensive support and passionate advocacy to individuals and self-advocates, their families, and surrounding natural supports throughout their communities. She considers herself a servant leader, one who cultivates, develops and maintains relationships with grace and grit in order to create, enhance, and promote services and programs that transform lives. On a personal level, her calling (not a career) allows her to give back some of what has so graciously been given to her family. She proudly serves as the Director of Family Support and Community Engagement at Achieving True Self, supporting families across the Northeastern U.S.

Living with her in that "boring" (ok, it's not actually boring) town and very much not boring household are her mother, forever known as "Mama Betty," her son, Christian, as well as Callie, Cookie, Candie, Hannah, Maddie, and Raven the furry felines -- that's right, six cats.

***

Connect with Catherine

The Caffeinated Advocate:
www.thecaffeinatedadvocate.com
Facebook: @caffeinatedadvocate
Instagram: @caffeinatedadvocate
LinkedIn: @catherineahughes
Pinterest: @caffeinatedadvocate
YouTube: The Caffeinated Advocate

CHAPTER 1:

Early Childhood And Preschool Memories, 1998–2002

My name is Christian Tomko, and I had a wonderful childhood. I am excited to share my history, my memories, and lessons learned in this book.

I was born on January 12, 1998. I was diagnosed with autism at a very young age (three). I have a great mother, whose name is Catherine, and a grandmother, whose name is Betty. My grandfather, John, passed away in 2009. I also have six cats named Callie, Cookie, Candie, Hannah, Raven, and Maddie (we have lost other cats along the way, and we lost our dog, Abby, in 2021).

During my childhood, I played with a bunch of toys; those toys included Legos, a "Thomas And Friends" train collection, "Pixar Cars," "Bob The Builder" vehicles, "Little People," and much, much more. I also watched many fantastic shows, which included *Sesame Street, Mister Rogers Neighborhood, Barney And Friends, Teletubbies, Bear In The Big Blue House, Arthur, The Wiggles, The Big Comfy Couch,* and a whole bunch more.

I have grown up with very friendly neighbors – Mike and Toni Henschel and their sons, Dan and Jonnie, Tom and Barbara (who sadly passed away) Rajchel and their boys, David and Jon (Peanut!), John and Ruth Brown, Marc and Debbie Gergely and their kids, Nicole, A.J., and Olivia. I got to know many more later in life when I delivered newspapers.

During those childhood years, I had some very awesome TSS, Therapeutic Support Staff, who helped me learn in spite of my diagnosis; some of those people included Jamie, Lillian, Emily, Karen, Dria, Melanie, Kristy, Christie, and so many more. I also had some helpful doctors along the way to help me with my overall health, along with managing my emotions – Dr. Faber, Dr. Newman (based at Mercy Hospital), and Dr. Chandra were just some of those doctors. My team and I did a lot of helpful but also fun things together. At the Children's Institute in the Shadyside area of Pittsburgh, I would usually see Dr. Faber, Kristy, or Melanie. Dr. Faber and Dr. Newman would oversee my health plans along with asking me what was going on in my everyday life. Kristy and Melanie would do some things similar to what the other two did at the Institute with me but they also taught me a lot. Kristy was my first occupational therapist and Melanie was my first speech therapist (Christie, in Monroeville, came later). While at home, ladies such as Jamie, Lillian, Dria, Karen, Emily and other people would come to my house, do some fun activities that also helped me learn, and watch fun TV shows during breaks. Sometimes they would come with me to the park to play, or go out to a fun restaurant to practice skills, or we would go to cool places that interested me. Jamie spent the most time with me – a few years.

When I was three and a half, I started going to preschool. My preschool was run by Project DART in Allegheny County, located in the Wallace Building in Baldwin, PA. Some of my favorite teachers included Miss Margaret, Miss Angie, Miss Debbie, and Miss JoHann. I also made a lot of great friends there, and met my very good friend Grace Nissen, mom to one of my preschool friends! Some of their activities included arts and crafts, snack and lunch time, recess, singing songs in the circle, and also included my very first costume parade during Halloween season. I was "Bob the Builder" and my costume looked great! I also had a very nice and pretty awesome bus driver whose name was Miss Marie.

At home, I enjoyed going next door and playing with Mike Henschel's two sons, Dan and Jonnie. The best part – I always loved jumping into their pool, going off the diving board, and going down the slide. They also had an adorable dog, Chloe (their other dog, Tasha, died when I was young).

I would also go over to Tom Rajchel's house and play with his two sons, David and Jon. Some fun things we did were playing basketball, playing hide and seek, going swimming together, and going on fun outings. I'll never forget when we went to a church event featuring Veggie Tales!

Sometimes, I would go to the Gergely's house and hang with A.J. We would go right onto the trampoline!

Other neighbors from time to time came over, like Rylee, who had "art class" with Lillian and I, and we would all play fun games together.

I am so thankful to be able to remember wonderful moments with such great people.

CHAPTER 2:

My Elementary Years, 2003–2006

When I was five years old, I was old enough to start kindergarten. I went to George Washington Elementary School in McKeesport, PA. I had a very nice kindergarten teacher, whose name is Karen Hronec. I also made a lot of very cool and awesome friends there; some of those many friends included Carl Cash, Bria Christian, Ciera Clifton, Niko Mallas, Anthony Fonzi, Chandlar Barfield, and Maniah Robinson. We did a lot of fun activities including circle time, playing on the computer, eating lunch together, and going outside for recess. Jamie was with me in kindergarten to support me if I needed help with anything. I also had a support teacher named Doreen Brooks, and I would visit her class throughout the day and do fun activities there during part of the day. I would ride the bus with her students in the morning and afternoon.

From 2004-2005, I had another very nice first grade teacher named Kelly McCloskey. I remember story time, having special guests from time to time, listening to music while doing our work, and we even learned how to make green eggs and ham! This is when I started seeing my first speech teacher, Mrs. Arbogast. Mrs. Arbogast would help me a lot with reading and other subjects. I really enjoyed drawing pictures for my first grade teacher. Some new friends I met included Cody Theis, Khalil White, and Ryder Lewis. I would sometimes go over to another table and draw when I needed to take a break. But I knew Mrs. McCloskey was always looking out for me throughout the day!

During that summer break, I attended a very awesome summer camp program called "Camp Chipewee," located at Mosside Middle School in Monroeville, PA. Jamie was with me throughout the day to assist me when I needed her. Monday through Thursday we would be at the camp (in a school) and do lots of fun activities like arts and crafts, singing songs together, playing inside the gymnasium, going outside and throwing water balloons, and sometimes we went on special field trips. Every Friday, we would go to Bel Aire Monroeville Community Pool, and I would have a blast jumping into the pool. At that time, I had my first swimming lessons with the lifeguard! Some of my favorite counselors were Jill, Amanda, Courtney, Brian, Sarah, Kristen, Jessica, and Mark (surely there were more). I also made a lot of good friends including Lee, Becky, Mary, Luke, Rhonda, and more, including my very good friend Taz Miller! I still have a photo of us from camp to remember those special days. The best part of camp though was spending time with all of my camp buddies and getting them all wet at the pool!

In 2005, I was in second grade, and had another nice teacher, Tamara Ekis. I remember doing a whole bunch of math problems back in those days! I remember when Mrs. Ekis showed us a picture of her daughter, Grace. Grace, sadly, passed away at a young age. Sometimes, I would go over and play with Legos in the corner when I needed time to calm down. I also met some cool people that year, including J.J. Doonan, Gavin Geissler, and Michael Walker. I also started seeing another speech therapist named Courtney Simon. Ms. Simon and I did a bunch of different activities, including learning about emotions, reading and writing properly, and being able to talk with her about my feelings.

During summer break after second grade, I went to another summer camp that Mrs. Brooks ran over at

Founders Hall Middle School as part of what is called Extended School Year (ESY). However, I didn't really stick with this program for a long time because something told me it just didn't fit my needs. But that's ok, because some things are just not for everyone. I did make some good friends though, including Michael Cheeseman, Danielle List, Mrs. Gallagher, Jessie Henry, James Thompson, and others. We also did some activities similar to those at my other camp like singing songs, going on field trips, throwing water balloons, and we would even have cookouts on days like Memorial Day or the Fourth of July. Even though I didn't stay there for long, I thought it was a really nice camp, and I am glad to keep those friendships no matter what happened.

In the year 2006 in third grade, I had a very awesome (ok, maybe the best!) teacher that I could ever imagine, and her name is Karen Bisi. Mrs. Bisi was always there for me no matter what, and she always had hilarious jokes right up her sleeve! Some of the activities we did were reading stories, doing math problems, writing cursive letters, and one time we did a cool project finding owl bones inside owl pellets. One of my favorite books I enjoyed there was "Trick Or Treat, Smell My Feet" – because I thought the title was so funny I just could not stop saying it over and over again.

I made even more nice friends there including Brent Murphy, Krystal Cella, Duane Tymous, Tina Williams, Arynn Pratt, Cameron Zuber, Bryan Gordon, Eric Brown, and so many more. I also met some other awesome teachers and even more people who touched my life; those people include Mrs. Smedley, Mr. Gwosden, Mr. Little, Mrs. Munoz, Mrs. Deak, Mrs. Ashbaugh, and many, many more. And who could forget the one and only Andrea Abrams? She was our principal and she, like Mrs. Bisi, is a part of my life to this day.

If I had to choose a few of my favorite memories of being at George Washington Elementary, one would be sitting in Mrs. Bisi's class smiling every day, another going out for the costume parade with our favorite band leader, and most of all, hearing Mrs. Smedley's good ol' laugh whenever anyone needed some cheering up.

CHAPTER 3:

My Grade School and Middle School Years, 2007–2012

I was about eight years old when I left George Washington Elementary. When summer break came to an end, I started attending Cornell Intermediate School, entering my fourth grade year. I had a very nice fourth grade teacher named Laurie Krall. In fourth grade I started to learn about science, history, and the math problems started to get a little harder! I also picked up my first instrument, which was the clarinet, and had a great band teacher named Chris Davidson. At one time in the school year, Mrs. Krall had to leave for a while due to personal things, and that is when I met my now very good friend Angela Elm. Mrs. Elm would also help me out when she came into the classroom, helping me with my day and helping to figure out what I needed to do on any given day. I also made some even more friends along the way, building even more relationships with people.

I had an awesome fifth grade teacher in 2008, Krystal Reid. I also learned some similar things in her class that I did in Mrs Krall's class. As I grew, I made more friends: Briana Alston, James Milton, Elijah McBride, Shawn Mackson, Nikoe Medina, Daaron Stinson, and a lot of other cool folks. My friend Elijah once taught me how to make a paper beak, and I thought that was so cool of him to teach me. I also made another friend, whose name is Brya Harper, and I remember the day she showed me her frog pen that croaked every time you pressed it. As soon as I pressed it, I could not stop laughing! My favorite part of that class was Mrs. Reid making all of us laugh when she started clowning around while teaching at the same time. She made learning fun!

2009–2010 brought sixth grade, which was also my final year at Cornell, and I had a wonderful teacher named Heather Amey. Mrs. Amey would always be proud of what I was doing, and she let me know that she was always there to help me, no matter what. I made some even more awesome friends including Malik Harrison, Thomas Vickovic, Dajour Leggett, Blake Flocker, Mark Cromerdie, and Eugene Davis.

When I was sitting in the group, Malik, the other boys, and I would always talk about and jam to "Big Time Rush." I also made two other friends, named Laquille and Teaira, who would think of really cool handshakes to do with me to make my day go even smoother! I was still in the band, and I met another awesome band teacher named Mr. DeCarlo.

As the sixth grade year was coming to an end, we heard the school building was going to be torn down, and we were all very sad! However, it was not going to be gone forever because a new school building would soon take its place, where new memories would be made. That school is now called Twin Rivers.

It was August 2010; summer was coming to an end, and I was leaving Cornell School and now coming upon my middle school years. I went to Founders Hall Middle School for my seventh and eighth grade years – until mid-2012. Things changed throughout those years because I was almost a teenager. Now I did not just have one class, I started in one class then went to others when the bell rang. I made even more friends in middle school like Paige Ellenberger, Michael Ritenour, Hayley Davis, Francesca Moux, Austin Ulm, Desmone Stanford, Dontae McCarthy, and a whole bunch of awesome young people. I also had a very nice

Individualized Education Plan (IEP) teacher named Mrs. Barnes, who would help me with my homework assignments and check in to see how my day was going. During my seventh grade year, I continued band class with Mr. DeCarlo and even got to be with my neighbor Jonnie Henschel, and I got to meet some more friendly students. Those people included Kaylin Johnson, Keshon Ball, Kayla DiMeo, Taylor Yester, Savanna Hardin, Hannah Jones, Casey Wash, and others. I also took new and ongoing classes like history, math, English, reading, cooking, music, and more.

During my eighth grade year, I continued to take band as a class and even played in concerts. During our final eighth grade concert, as we were about to announce the eighth grade award before playing the last song, the winner was announced and that winner happened to be me! I am proud to say that I was good at playing the clarinet then – and I still continue to be today. I love music!

I also joined a small social group during that time with a school psychologist, named Miss Phelps, along with some friends like Braxton Schierer, Aaron Crews, Michael Cheng, and my very good friend Michael Permigiani, whom I have known for a very long time.

I then met another great IEP teacher named Mrs. Gault; she would help me out with difficult situations and help me with my homework assignments throughout the day when I needed it.

Every Friday during homeroom period, I would go see Miss Phelps and talk to her about what was going on with me and we would figure out some ways to cope with my emotions and situations and how to make things better. Everyone took a field trip to White Oak Pool to celebrate our last day of the eighth grade year.

My favorite moment during my Founders Hall years would definitely have to be riding around with my neighbor Jonnie, along with some of his friends like Tyler Cook, Emily Druskin, Steve Mandella, Carly Sherer, Mary Pearce, Jim Kiss, and others who also befriended me. Grateful for the good times!

CHAPTER 4:

The High School Years, 2013–2016

In 2013, I entered my freshmen year, and I was now a teenager. I headed to McKeesport Area High School. My days of playing the clarinet in the band came to an end; I decided that I really needed more time to focus on my homework. That year I met my IEP teacher Sherri Geyer, who was my IEP teacher throughout my high school years.

As the school years went by, the subjects got much harder, but I did make even more friends throughout the year. I met my favorite guidance counselor, George Lepsch, who was always so supportive of me and always helped me when I needed someone to talk to (along with Mrs. Geyer of course). I had an awesome history teacher, whose name is Ed Hrinda. He had two very cool speeches – a morning and a headline test speech, that he would always repeat as soon as he walked into the class, or whenever there was a headline test. I remember he would put on some Pink Floyd while we were taking the tests.

In my freshman year, I met some more awesome friends including Josh Peters, R.J. Harris, Alex Morgan, Daniel Nicholson, David Orosz, Lyle Petrosky, Jenna Frum, and Khaleke Hudson (and, if you're a Washington Redskins fan, his name is familiar to you!). Jonnie had moved on to Serra Catholic High School in White Oak, however I did meet a bunch of his friends including Nate Haight, Nate Guzewicz, Chris Beech, Joe Driscoll, Zach Thielet, and many more, and we also had the chance to hang out now and then, even though we attended different schools.

In the year 2014, I was a sophomore and the subjects started to get even harder. I had a wonderful English teacher named Jennifer Hairston. She was always there for me and would help me whenever I needed extra assistance in any way. After her class, I had a very cool math teacher named Robert Hartnett (God rest his soul; he sadly passed away in 2020). He would always play cool music videos on YouTube. He introduced me to Joe Satriani, Jimi Hendrix, and Stevie Ray Vaughan. I also enjoyed biology with Marla Hayes. Every Monday and Tuesday, we would have lab every seventh period, and we did fun science experiments.

One time we even learned to dissect frogs – unfortunately, I ended up tearing mine to shreds!

I also met Jahsai Allen, Will Spencer, Jake Stumpf, Matt Pietraz, Josh Steele, Tymar Sutton, Dana Coles, and more friendly folks. My very favorite part of the sophomore year though was taking swimming class in the last semester. I learned new swim techniques from Mrs. Burgh.

In 2015, I began my junior year and was not too far from graduating high school. I had a very cool – and hilarious! – science teacher named Mr. Bauman. One of the funniest moments I remember was when Mr. Bauman logged onto YouTube and played "The Pancreas Song." I also met some more cool people like Sidney Satterfield, Jessica Washowich, Meghan Lewis, and my very best friend Amy Wargo.

I also had a very cool history teacher named Mrs. Halfhill; she was always so helpful to me and knew when I was in need of extra support. In that class, I met my friend Hillary Whatley; I always enjoyed joking around with her throughout the day. I also had a funny Writing Studio teacher named Mr. O'Conner; he was always clowning around and making the whole classroom laugh while he was teaching. My favorite part of my junior year, however, was being able to learn right from wrong; Mrs. Geyer and Mr. Bauman helped me with truly embracing those differences. I appreciated that.

I went to my first high school prom in my junior year with my good friend Kaylee Holtzman. I also was inducted into the National Honor Society – that focus on my homework paid off!

In 2015, I entered my senior year and graduation time was getting close (June 2016). Outside of school, this was the year when I got my first part time job, working at Puzzlers, in the small town of Christy Park, as a busboy. Puzzlers was founded by a wonderful family, the Osinskis, who proudly support autism efforts.

I also started working with a counselor from the PA Office of Vocational Rehabilitation (OVR) named Andrew Rossi, whose job it was to help me find the right college and the appropriate job for me one day. I also had a great Sociology teacher, Mr. Shank, who was so hilarious I could not stop laughing in his classes. I met Ryan Luketic, Nate and Devin Mulvay, Mike LaRotonda, Harlie McKelvey, Kylie Thielet, Dalana Gebis, and more. I had a very cool math teacher named Mr. Hegedus, who always told me if you have a question, just ask. I'll never forget that!

My favorite class of all was psychology class with Mr. Szymczak. There, I met my good friend Kayle Lovell, and Casey Harbert, Brian Davis, Alexa Kent, and Selena McCurdy amongst others. One of my favorite moments in that class was learning about Jean Piaget and his sensory motor stage. One of Piaget's examples was object permanence and the game "peekaboo." I thought it sounded fun. I ended up playing along with one of the other girls, and then with Kayle. Then the teacher ended up repeating it to me. I just had to laugh along, and I could not stop. I remember walking down the hall at the end of the day once, and I saw Kayle, who then played peekaboo right back at me!

I also made good friends at lunch that year like Teddi Williams, Maddie Gradich, Carlie Hornfeck, Kyle Nelson, Riley Perciavalle, and another one of my favorite friends, Jacey Mirenna. Jacey was always so kind to me at lunch, and she would always make silly faces at me whenever I had fun joking with her. Kyle, Riley, and I would also have fun jamming at the lunch table to different songs, and we would have a blast. At the end of lunch, Teddi, Maddie, and Carlie would not stop flirting with me and had me blushing until my cheeks turned red! Then Mr. Pressel would walk in and our crew would start joking around and call him "Soft Pressel." He would pretend to put me in a headlock!

I went to my senior prom with my kindergarten teacher's daughter, Jordyn Hronec. That night was such a blast, because I got to take pics with all of my good friends and dance with everyone! I also won a senior superlative during Senior Projects, Class Flirt (all those surprised?). Before graduation, I also won two scholarships, one of which was from the White Oak Rotary Club and the other was the Justin R. Misura Memorial Award. I remember saying at each ceremony that I wanted to someday give back to my community, and I truly wanted to be remembered as a person with autism in the hope that people would understand what I went through to become the man I am today.

Not long after, that proud moment came when we got to put on our caps and gowns and receive our diplomas. I graduated with High Honors, and wore a silver cord, just like my mom! My very favorite, one of the best moments yet, was being able to walk across that stage, receive my diploma, and proudly graduate from high school.

I was hoping that I would be able to keep in touch with most of my friends and teachers, even though we all may move on in life. So far, I've done pretty good!

CHAPTER 5:

The College And Work Years, 2017– Present Day

I officially graduated high school, and it was time to move onto bigger and better things. During the summer before college, I had my very own high school graduation party, thrown by family and friends. We had a lot of people there, tons of food, and even some karaoke with my good friend DJ April! I was still working at Puzzlers as a busboy, and made a lot of cool friends like Chuck Kepple, Amber Cooke, Amber Peebly, Kristie Olinsky, Chaz Margliotti, Brenda and Joe Osinski, and even got to work with my friend Reco Crawford from school.

I soon found a second part-time job at The New Buster's Pizza and Cream. At this job, I made new friends, such as Susan and Chuck Readel (the owners), Amanda Wieghan, Tim Mient, Jenn Kirby, Dan Kovic, and more. I had a lot of different duties at Buster's, but my main job at Puzzlers was to help wash the dishes and make sure they were clean and sanitized. My favorite part at both jobs was having fun and messing around with all my coworkers. I like to have a good time while I work, just like when I was at school. My funniest memories of Puzzlers were when Chaz would clown around and try to sneak up on me during my breaks. It was also at Puzzlers that I discovered my love of karaoke!

In August 2016, I started my first day of college, pursuing a career in culinary arts. The first college I went to was CCAC Allegheny Campus on the North Side of Pittsburgh. However, I didn't really last long there, and did not make too many friends there. I had a rough time. But at least I gave it my best shot and made at least one good friend named Ksenia Shaw. I continued seeing my therapist, Sarah Benson, who would help me cope with my emotions, think of new ways to deal with difficult situations, and teach me how to get along with my family better.

In 2017, I decided to try out for another post-secondary program as part of a program called Police And Fire Academy (PFA) in the North Hills section of Pittsburgh. They offered a vocational food service program there. I made a few friends, and I did an excellent job cooking. I did have a few issues there as well, and this program also turned out to not be what was best for me. However, that was OK because like the old saying goes, college is not for everyone. I moved on and sought out a new job.

In 2018, I started working at the White Oak Giant Eagle, not too far from my house. I also got my first job coach from Goodwill Industries, Matt Langille. Matt would check up on me at my job, talk about ways to improve, and meet with me later to find other jobs. At Giant Eagle, I first started off in the deli, working in the hot foods department, completing many different duties like food prep, serving customers, and smashing down cardboard. But things didn't really work out well, so I tried being a front end cashier. Up there I would make sure the money in the drawer was not over or short, check out customers, and make sure the customers would leave with smiles on their faces. However, I did not last there due to some personal issues. Matt, Andrew, and I started to talk about different job opportunities that would possibly fit me better.

Late in 2018, I started to work at Dollar General as a stock person, as well as a front end cashier. I met some more friendly people including Laura Belko,

Jermaisha Pratt (who I went to school with), Sam Miller, and my good man Jaime Brown. Jaime would always help to make my days better, teach me how to do the right thing, and teach me how to treat customers the way they deserved to be treated. There were often times when Laura called me when someone was needed. There were times that I was not sure if I wanted to come in; however, I believed that work came first and that I should always help someone when needed. I really enjoyed working with Sam because she would always clown around with me while working. However, it was not long after (maybe a few months) when another job opportunity came along and my time at Dollar General came to an end.

I then took a position at Apple Harvest Catering, located in North Versailles. I thought this job would be a great opportunity to take my cooking skills to the next level. However, this job did not last long, and I left after a thumb injury.

I was thinking about going back to Dollar General, but I was not sure what I wanted to do. So then I finally decided maybe I just needed a break from working to figure out what to do next, and then I found my first volunteer gig at Kane Regional Centers in McKeesport, where my grandpa was a patient before

31

he passed away. This is also where I would visit my good friend Frank Simonetta, help the residents with activities (like bingo), and transport them to and from church, and have lunch with the volunteer workers.

Also noteworthy, that year is that I started going to the first church I chose called Calvary Baptist Church in West Mifflin, and there, I experienced a baptism. And then, something awesome happened. I obtained my driver's license after a year of practice. Shoutout to Todd from A1 Driving School! A week after I passed, I got my first vehicle, a 2016 Jeep Patriot (funny thing is, it looked just like my mom's old car!).

It was 2019, and I met a lot of friendly people like Barry Mang, Ed Faircloth, Cruz Quezada, Marsha Fairbanks, Shayla Lofton, and even got to work with my friend Raykel Smith with whom I graduated. Next thing you know I had volunteered myself into a job at Kane, working in the kitchen!

When I worked the morning shift, I started out part-time and still was not working many days. I remember talking to Sharon Littlejohn, and I soon accepted my first full time position and experienced what it was like working a full shift. I felt so nervous, and then depression just hit me. I did not know what was going on. But I knew I needed to do something to make myself happier. I liked the people, but I realized maybe the kitchen was not the right place for me for a job (maybe a hobby!) and, perhaps, maybe I needed to pursue another career. I stayed until mid 2020.

I took a test and was awarded a City Carrier Assistant position with the post office in the summer of 2020, which was also about the time when the COVID–19 pandemic hit. I remember the day I was trying out all of the mail vehicles, and I had no idea I would be driving on the opposite side of the vehicle. I struggled and learned that I automatically failed the test, and, unfortunately, the people ended up letting me go. Around this time my OVR and job coaching cases came to a close. They knew I was such a hard worker, and that I now had the skills to find something that would fit me. I interviewed for different jobs during the summer after that, but I had no luck finding anything. By August, I got help from mom's good friend Michelle Tomchek. She suggested a place called Milestone's. I was soon interviewed at Milestone by a wonderful program director, whose name is Paula Fisher. Next thing you know, I got the job.

When I first started at Milestone's, I met some great coworkers including Justin Bushman, Angela Schwanke, Chris Pitt, and Dylan Straw. I thought to myself, wow, this job could be the career of my lifetime. I did start to have some struggles along the way, but everyone told me that I always did a good job, and they reminded me that you can always ask for something when you need help (remember my teacher who taught me "all you need to do is ask"). It was in Fall 2020 when I realized things with COVID were starting to get much worse, and that's when we were told our day program was going to be shut down until it was safe to go back. I knew it was not going to be forever, but I felt sad because I also heard Angela, Chris, and Dylan were leaving. I knew they would still visit from time to time, though.

It was now Spring 2021, and the program had just opened back up. I met some new friendly workers like Mike Stead, Tammie Kay, and Annie Grimm. As I continued my work there, the job got much harder. But I knew the staff, including Paula, were always there for me when I was in need of a hand. My favorite parts of the job are getting to give lessons, helping the clients, taking them on community outings, and I do especially love having weekends and holidays off! Sometimes I bring my guitar in, and I offer singalongs with the clients.

We've reached 2022, and I am still working at Milestone. I was having a bunch of struggles here and there at the beginning of the year. Annie asked how everything was with me, I told her how I felt, and this is when she suggested having weekly check-ins with me to see how everything was going. This was a great idea! Justin would also help me out and talk to me about how important it is to work as a team, and he taught me something valuable – that not everything is about me. Mike would tell me that I should always have confidence in myself, always be professional, and to always be alert when something is happening in a situation. I was so worried about losing this job I loved, so Paula and her assistant Kaitlyn now join in the check-ins along with Annie, so I really can make this job the career of a lifetime (remember, I said I wanted to help my community!) and be successful. The most important things I have learned about having a job, I would say, are to always be on time, act professional, be kind, and to always leave with a smile on your face.

CHAPTER 6:

Adulthood, Present Day

I am now 24 years old, and I am still living with my mother and grandmother. But I know one day there will be a greater opportunity for maybe owning my own house – once I make enough money, and I know I need to save as much as I can.

I have never had a girlfriend, which makes me very, very sad. But I have faith that one day I will meet the girl that is looking for me, maybe get married, and have a wonderful family. As another old saying goes, there are plenty of fish out there in the sea.

Last year, I thought that maybe Calvary Baptist was not the church for me. So I found another one called Bridge City Church that my friend Mary Shelly suggested I try out. The church has two services, and I enjoy going to both. Sometimes we even do outdoor services located at Monroeville Park, and we have fun outdoor activities. A lot of friends I went to school with go there as well, including Jimmy Young, Nicole Lakovic and her sister Marissa, Canaan Baldinger and his family, Morgan and Joe Cohen, and even my neighbor Tom Rajchel (a pastor) from the North Braddock location. Sometimes we would even do church groups run by different pastors and men like Jim Armstrong, Rob Benadetti, Jeff Roerhig, my friend Taylor Yester's dad Paul, Rick Paladin, and the main White Oak pastor Nick Stephanovic.

I now play a couple of different instruments like the guitar, keyboard, bongos, and even the bass. I also received a clarinet this past Christmas from my family so I can play that again, too! I also recently bought myself a didgeridoo. Whenever I start to feel down, I will go downstairs, turn on the amp, plug my guitar in, and start playing along. I even know how to teach myself how to play all kinds of different types of songs. My favorite types of music these days are classic rock, heavy metal, oldies, jazz, and holiday music. I will listen to anything in those genres, but not rap. I even know how to fix a broken guitar string myself!

Since starting my job at Milestone's, I enjoy doing crafts and I think they are so much fun. I decided to give arts and crafts a try as a hobby. I still love to draw, but now I am getting more artistic. I love to make seasonal crafts; however, my favorite crafts are holiday crafts, because I always have the holiday spirit when it comes to a favorite holiday! I even started to make beaded name bracelets for all of my good friends. You never know, maybe one day I will start hosting my own bracelet sales.

At the end of 2020, our favorite next door neighbors, the Henschels, permanently left Pennsylvania and moved to Colorado to start their very own business. I was very sad when they told me that they were moving away. However, I knew this was not a forever goodbye because I knew I could always FaceTime them when I needed to talk to someone. I also hope one day, when I have more vacation time off, I can face my fears and get on an airplane to fly out and see the neighbors I care for so much. I still talk to the Henschels on FaceTime, along with their good friends Caleb Shively, Jason Brletic, and I also met their good friends Wade Harger and Johnny Wolfe. I even will have "sessions" sometimes with Mike's very good friend Bruno Vick. Bruno is always there for me in a heartbeat. He helped me out whenever I felt depressed; he still does to this day.

CHAPTER 7:

More Memorable Moments From My Life, Past and Present

I have a lot of great memories of people, whether family, neighbors, or just good people. Here's some more special moments from my life in no particular order.

I remember during the summer of 2021 when I was invited to Henschel's pool to go swimming with all of their friends for a going away party. Some of those people included Rachael Jacklitch, Taylor Potts, Colton Joseph, Luke Blacka, Jaron Dormarsky, Pete Smerecky, Marty Slovonic, and more. We had lots of food, enjoyed music, and there were so many games to play. My favorite game was beer pong – even though I ended up drinking iced tea. Another funny moment I remember was when Rachael came up behind me and pretended to put me in a headlock.

I remember the time I went out to dinner with my family along with Mrs. Bisi, Mrs. Abrams, and Mrs. Smedley, before she, sadly, passed away. We all went to Woody's in McKeesport (long before the restaurant caught fire and closed down). The ladies showered me with many great gifts to make me happy, which was very kind. I really enjoyed sitting with Mrs. Smedley and hearing her laugh. Everyone loved her laugh! We all sat down and talked about all the good times that we had at George Washington Elementary and then ordered some yummy Italian dinner. I will never forget that wonderful moment together, and I can still hear Mrs Smedley's laugh right now.

During the summer, I learned that my good friend Jacey was leaving for college, and I was so upset. So we did a late lunch / early dinner date to Buca Di Beppo down at Station Square in Pittsburgh. I told her how much I was going to miss her. I was about ready to cry! But I knew it was not going to be forever, and I was just hoping to see her again soon. But then times went by, and we went our separate ways. However, I know Jacey is still my friend, and I know I will get to see her again one day.

I went to my first Halloween party in the fall of 2021. This was also my first time going to an awesome art studio called Brand Name Glass in the East Liberty section of Pittsburgh. I also got to finally meet now great friend Gian Oliver who owns the place. I saw Chris Beech, Sam Whitney, Sam Campbell, and so many other great people. For this party, I dressed up as Oscar The Grouch and went up to people pretending to be Oscar from *Sesame Street*. I also got to experience some of the cool artwork that Gian and some of the other guys do at Brand Name Glass.

I have been to so many birthday parties over the years, however the best party I have ever been to was in remembrance of my good man Austin Fagan. We had lots of food, music, gave bracelets to friends, and the best part was releasing the balloons in the air in memory of Austin. I also got to see my wonderful friends Jamie Grayson, Dylan Ernst, Nick Howard, Tomi McKelvey, Jason Chavis, and so many more. I even got to make a couple of bucks while giving away some of my bracelets! It is so very sad when one of your good friends passes away, but you can still remember them everyday.

I love to do special things for my birthday and go to many fun restaurants. One time, my mom threw me a party at Woody's. However things did not seem to go my way because I was not expecting this to happen. I learned I just didn't like surprise parties! But Mike Henschel was there to help me make things better, and as the saying goes, turn lemons into lemonade. This year (2022), I would say was definitely the best birthday I ever could have imagined! I turned my birthday into what some people may sometimes call a birthday week! I kind of made it go a little longer than that because I had a lot of things planned this year. Let me share more.

First, I went into work, and I received a lot of awesome gifts from my friends and coworkers; then at home we ordered dinner from Twin Oaks, and finally got to eat cake and ice cream and open all of my presents from mom and grandma. The second day, I went out to dinner at Texas Roadhouse, where I met my good friend Christian Harris, and everyone came out to give me a big Roadhouse "Yee–Haw!" The week after, I went back to Buca Di Beppo with my wonderful friend Alicia Howard, who I met working at Giant Eagle, and we ordered some awesome Italian food. The day after that I went to an awesome breakfast place that I enjoy going to a lot called First Watch in Baldwin, where my longtime friend Amy Wargo works, and I celebrated with a good breakfast and a glass of Purple Haze. In February (I told you I extended the celebration!) I went out to an awesome Mexican restaurant called Plaza Azteca, right next to the church I go to along with my friends Evan Reed, Jeremy Kiger, and his girlfriend Morgan, and two of his friends. At the end everyone came out and put the Mexican hat right on my head and sang "Happy Birthday" to me in Spanish. I think the best part about having birthdays is when you get to choose where you would like to go and do fun things with family and friends who love you.

I am someone who loves to have fun and joke around. Well in April we had a very awesome show at Brand Name Glass called "April With Some Fools." There were so many great people, including my friend Melanie Mills, Rob Geddy, and Gian's girlfriend, Miley. I ended up bringing in and coming up with as many April Fools Day pranks that I could think of. So I said at first that no one could fool me on that day. Well, it turned out that a few people there proved me wrong, big time. I ended up "April Fooling" a whole bunch of people, so a few of the people ended up getting back at me. One guy ended up taking my pile of plastic dog poop and put it in the freezer till it froze! I also ended up putting sticky notes on people's backs and Mel ended up giving me bunny ears after that. The funniest part was when Miley took the note, smashed it, and tried to give me "the boot" afterwards. I also had fun getting everyone with my gas blaster and blasting everyone in the face.

I remember many years ago, that my mom, her boyfriend, Dave, and his son, Brenden, and I all took a trip out to a park in PA called Ohiopyle. We all walked around and saw so many beautiful things. We even went into the water and relaxed by the waterfalls. But we couldn't go swimming because we did not have our swimsuits with us that day. Other than that, it was a fabulous time, and I hope to go out again one day with one of my friends.

I loved going to the autism fundraising walks when I was younger, and I enjoyed helping out when I could. I also went to another autism walk with our good friends Meghan and Kevin Minich. There I met the famous David Newell, who played Mr. McFeely on *Mister Rogers Neighborhood*. We met and even got an autograph from him; he wrote his catchphrase "Speedy Delivery!" At another one of the walks, I got to see my friend Kayle and her friends Kayla Lopez and Kyle Marracini. We all hung out, took the walk, watched the band play, and had a wonderful time together. One time at a community awards event for my mom, I was at PNC Park and met famous football coach Herman

Boone. I shook hands with him, and even got to take a picture with him.

I continue to pray that I continue to experience more wonderful moments, and to build even more meaningful friendships throughout my life.

CHAPTER 8:

More About My Accomplishments Over The Years

Over the years, I have worked to better my many talents and have experienced many accomplishments. One of my biggest struggles that I deal with is both my mental and physical health. So to help with that, I visit a few doctors: I have my psychiatrist, my chiropractor, and my therapist. I tend to see two psychiatrists from time to time, Dr. Slezak and Dr. Orr. Each one of their schedules is different. I go in for the check up first, and then I will talk with whomever is available that day, and talk to them about what is going on with my health, any family issues, or what I can do to move forward. I have seen them for a long time now and still continue seeing them as of this day.

I have a very cool new primary care physician (PCP) that I see; his office is not too far from my house.

His name is Dr. Jurewicz. Dr Jurewicz is very helpful and gives me really great advice on what is healthy and what is not. He also suggested a low carb diet for me to try. I am working now to really slim down. I am really focusing on eating more proteins, veggies, and keeping carbs low – not just to eat healthier, but to feel happier.

I am also going to a gym called "Blue Line Fitness" in the Christy Park section of McKeesport. Each day, I will do a different section of body parts along with a little bit of abs along with cardio. Sometimes I will walk around the block in our neighborhood, go to one of the parks near my house, or do one of my friend's workout videos for a rest day.

I really would love to become a better guitar player one day. I have had many jam sessions with a few of my friends like Kyle Styche, Kris Gamble, and Michael Ritenour. Each one of them teaches me and shows me how to really get my strumming pattern going. Kyle also once showed me how to fix a guitar string, so I know what I need to do when I need to fix one that is broken. Mike even taught me how to play the bass, which isn't as hard as an acoustic guitar. He even gave me his Paul McCartney bass as a Christmas gift in 2020. That was amazing, and I was so excited. Kris once showed me some cool videos of how Lindsay

Buckingham and Jack Sonni play guitar without using a pick. I pray that one day I will become a master at playing. I will continue to take time to practice even more and take things one step at a time.

Weekly after work, I see my therapist, Ryan Delaney. I have been seeing Ryan for a while now, and he is, maybe, one of the best therapists that I have ever had of all my outpatient therapists. I go into the office, talk to Ryan about what's going on in my life, and he gives me ways to deal with tough situations. The best advice Ryan has ever given me is to always use a deep breathing method whenever I start to feel depressed or hopeless. I could never imagine any other therapist as good as Ryan.

A little after New Year's Day, and a little before my birthday, I went to Brand Name Glass to take my very first glassmaking class. Gian and Chris showed me how to make glass pendants to hang on necklaces. It is very complicated and can be very dangerous, but it can be so much fun at the same time. Luckily, Gian was there to help me. Gian explained that you always keep the glass in the flame no matter what, keep rotating it at all times, and then, the fun part is, you can pick whatever color you like. I made two pendants for my necklace, one that was red and blue and another that was black and yellow. I even got to take some pendants home for my mom and grandma! You never know what things Gian and his staff will come up with when it comes to making glass.

This spring, I have found a new hobby that I really enjoy which is going fishing. With the help of my great friend Kirk Sandusky, and his friend Noah Culp, I got my rods all fixed up and ready to go. Kirk also explained to me the right kind of bait to use for catching each type of fish. Fishing is really relaxing and really fun, but it also takes some patience while you are waiting for the fish to bite. Some of the places I like to fish are Lake Emilie at Renzie and Indian Lake in North Huntingdon. So far I have caught a few trout, a bluegill, and a crappie. One day, I hope to really become an expert at fishing and maybe try to fish out on the river and maybe do some night fishing with a couple folks.

If I had to name one of my best accomplishments yet, it would have to be learning how to cook more at home. My grandma has been struggling a lot due to her health, so I decided to try and take over in the kitchen a bit to help her out with cooking when she needs extra help. I am someone who loves to cook for myself, my family, the people I work with, and hopefully one day some of my friends! Some of the things I love to cook are breakfast buffet foods, Italian, Mexican, and foods on the grill. I have learned how to cook a whole meal for Thanksgiving, Christmas, and Easter. Ever since I started using Pinterest, I started looking up lots of new and fascinating recipes for the holidays, or simply for any other day that I feel like cooking. My family, friends, and the people I work with really enjoy my cooking.

I am extremely proud of all the accomplishments I have made over the years, and I will continue to make more while I move on in life.

CHAPTER 9:

A Few More Accomplishments and Memories

When I was in school, I was so nervous to get up on stage in front of everyone! As soon as I got up on stage in front of everyone, tears came falling down my face. I didn't know what to do because I was so worried about what people were going to say or do. But as I grew up, I learned to face my fears, and I became less nervous and became a pro at getting up on stage! I now have the guts to get up on any stage at any time to offer whatever talent I have, even in front of a huge audience. I even spoke to a high school audience a year after graduating about my experiences. It was wonderful, and I hope to do it again someday.

It was during Thanksgiving season in the year 2020; my friend Caleb Shively and I headed out to his friend's studio where they all hang out and play music.

I walked into the studio and thought to myself, "Wow, this is so amazing." I then fearlessly hopped up on stage, and we all performed some awesome songs. I sang into the microphone a few times and even played guitar. Caleb and his brother Marc were right there next to me to help me out. But I was not scared at all! It was such an awesome experience to get up on stage and see what it is like to jam with a group of people.

I remember when I went on "The Missions Trip" and had such a blast. I made some more friends including Jessica Hotujec and her husband Nick, Randy Young, and more. First we all met at the church, and then we all went down to Christy Park and helped weed whack the area to make McKeesport look nice and clean. After our hard work, we all went down to Rita's for some good ol' Italian Ice. Then we all went down to the North Braddock location for the final service to hear the good word, and then we went home. One day, I hope to join them for the Memorial Day Parade they do every year in White Oak.

It was February 2022, a little after Valentine's Day, and I went to Brand Name Glass to see a local favorite performer, Happy Clouds, do a live show. I got to see all of my friends, took some pictures, and even participated in a raffle contest there! So, after I grabbed my food, a friend of Gian's gave me a ticket with a number on it. Whose number would be called after the performance would be the winner. Then one of the guys went up and called the winning number, and my number happened to be called. I was the winner of the contest! Happy Clouds gave me some of his stickers that he collects as a cool gift.

In past Halloweens, I volunteered at the Haunted Hills Hayride in North Versailles. I love Halloween so much, so I thought I would give it a try, and I did. The team then put fake blood on my face and my job was to go where I was assigned and scare people! That is one of my most favorite parts of Halloween. I decided that maybe volunteering there was not for me, but that will never stop me from visiting, seeing my good friends, and getting a good scare on Halloween!

I am also hoping one day to maybe turn my bracelet hobby into a money making venture (cash I could really use!). So I went to see my good friend Jonathon Cornell to visit his vendor show, and he suggested I should try out his bracelet sale to gather my thoughts. I thought his bracelets looked so cool, and I decided to get some Mother's Day gifts for my mom and grandma. I know if I take the time to really make more of a variety of bracelets, I will definitely be ready to join him or maybe do a sale of my own. The best part of giving and receiving gifts is making each other happy. Sometimes the best gifts do come in small packages!

CHAPTER 10:

Learning Experiences and My Final Notes

I have learned and experienced a lot throughout my life. My mom and grandma have taught me a whole lot throughout my childhood and into my adult years now. Now I have had a lot of conflict with the two of them; however, no matter how much we may argue from time to time, you still have to honor your family, no matter what. Sometimes I don't understand why mom or gram gets upset. I will usually think it is at me, but such is not the case at times. Everyone gets upset once in a blue moon – we all have our good days and our bad days.

One day at Camp Chipewee, when I was a child, we all went on a field trip to Kennywood. We went on most of the rides we wanted to go on. It was not long after when we all finished eating that I wanted to ride even more rides. It was not long after that I accidentally got lost. Everyone started to worry and wondered where I was. Luckily, I was found, but folks were not happy with what I did. Life lesson learned – it is ok to have fun, but, when you're with a huge group, you must stay with the group. People will worry about you!

I am also experiencing a lot of my friends getting married, having kids, or moving away. There are a lot of times I will get so jealous when I see my friends getting married, and I don't understand why. Sometimes when people are going out with each other, they just want to be with that certain person; they need privacy at times, and like to go on dates by themselves! But friends have told me that it is definitely not worth getting jealous or upset over a friend getting married. If someone or one of your friends is getting married, you should always be happy for that person no matter what! The key to success is to be happy and have confidence in *yourself*, always.

There is a song by The Rolling Stones titled "You Can't Always Get What You Want." Well, I tend to struggle – a lot – when things don't go my way. I will say that I have learned, and truly embraced recently, that not everything is about me and that I have to learn to do what other people like to do. There were a few occasions that my friends and I originally had something planned and then things got changed. Sometimes those types of changes can make me very upset, maybe a little too upset. It sucks when your original plan does not work out; however, if plan A does not work, then that's when you go to plan B. I have realized that you have to learn to take turns, and it is ok to try new and exciting things.

I am someone who loves to go out and be with people, but sometimes I can get a little nervous. Sometimes I will ask people to hang out, but you cannot always expect it to happen because someone might not be available; things happen. When I cannot get my way, when I feel like people don't have time for me, I tend to get very depressed and lonely. Luckily, with the help of my friend George Stepansky, I've learned that when no one is available to hang, I can maybe use that time to take time for myself and reset my mind. At first I was not sure about it, but as soon as I got in the car and drove off that day, I thought, "maybe it is ok to have fun by yourself sometimes." I really do love hanging with my friends, but everyone is allowed to take some time to themselves when they need it – including me.

A final note about one of the most important lessons I have learned in my life: lately, I have had struggles with people moving on. I was worried it was because some people were upset with me, or they did not like me anymore, or they did not want to be my friend anymore. However, I know all of that is absolutely not true. I know I have a lot of great people who care about me. You should only stick with those people that you are close to, that you can trust, and think about who is really your friend. This is great advice for anyone! I was curious at some point as to why people were not returning my messages. But a lot of people have told me that just because someone doesn't reply to you right away does not mean that person is ignoring you. They are right. Remember this! It is important to realize that after you graduate, people may fade away. But that does not mean those certain people are not your friends. I also learned you can still be friends with people, but should not try too hard to make an effort to hang with that certain person. A few people have told me that someone can still be my friend, even though they get busy due to jobs, marriages, and kids. I have been so busy myself that I, too, have tended to have a lack of contact with other people. But that's ok.

No matter how busy people get and fade away, I know that I have many friends who have touched my life, and I can still cherish those memories that I had and still have of them from this day forth.

I have loved looking back at all of my memories and hope you have enjoyed reading them. As my good friend Mr. Hegedus would say, food may be done, and this story of my life to date is now finished.

About The Author

Christian Tomko is the author of *A Milestone Journey: Memories And Lessons Throughout The Years*. He has lived in White Oak, PA for all of his life, currently with his mother, grandmother, and his six cats. His mother and grandmother, Catherine Hughes and Betty C. Tomko assisted with the editing of this book. Both ladies actually have authored and edited other books, including a posthumous publication of his grandfather's poetry. This is the first book Christian has ever written, and he clearly comes by writing naturally! Christian also likes to journal when he needs time to himself and enjoys writing chords and learning new songs. Other hobbies include karaoke, working out, crafting, and fishing. Christian is very proud of what he has done throughout his young life, and is looking forward to new experiences as his life moves on.

The author can be contacted through The Caffeinated Advocate or Grace & Hope Consulting, LLC:
chughes@thecaffeinatedadvocate.com
chou@graceandhopeconsulting.com

PHOTO GALLERY

These photos I am sharing are in no particular order, but I do hope you enjoy seeing some of my favorite memories – and people!

Me and Joe Driscoll at Blue Line Fitness getting our daily workout in for the day.

Me, Caleb Shively, brothers Noah and Marc, and their friend Dustin, gambling at the Rivers Casino.

Me and my friends Tomi McKelvey, Tyler Cook, Dylan Ernst, and Nick Howard gathered outside of Renzie Park in memory of our friend Austin Fagan. I was so surprised when Tyler threw up the bunny ears right behind my head. I should have known that was coming!

Me, and Austin Fagan's mother Danean smiling and remembering the good times at the party we threw for Austin.

Me, Nicole Gergely, and Carly, posing in front of the camera after an award ceremony.

Me and Libby Baldinger at my graduation party.

Me and Libby Baldinger's sister Nicole.

Me and my best friend Niko Mallas; I have known him for a very long time.

Me and some of my favorite teachers posing for the camera at my graduation party. Here standing with me are Mrs. Marcie Barry, Mrs. Kris Nemchick, Mrs. Marsha Bauer, Ms. Joy Turek, and last, but most certainly not least, Mrs Sherri Geyer.

Me and my very good friend Eric Buczynski partied at my graduation celebration.

Me and my favorite neighbors, the Henschels! (Mike and his son Jonnie on the left, his wife Toni, and other son Dan on the right). Mike would always be there to help me out in a heartbeat, no matter what the situation. I always thought of them as my other family, and still do to this day.

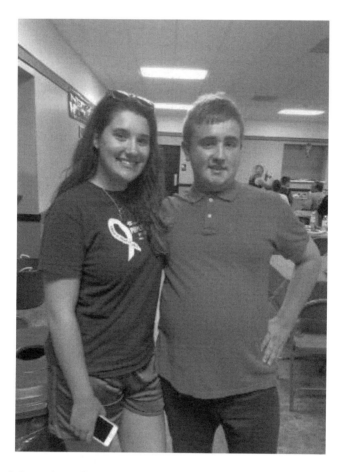

Me and my "bestest" friend Jacey Mirenna smiling for the camera.

Me and my friends Jacey Mirenna, Kylie Thielet, Jenna Blair, and her friend Chris standing in front of the camera.

Me and friend Michael Cheeseman, his mother Jeanne, and her husband Tim Locke posing for the camera. My favorite part is when Tim mentions "Railroad" because he is also a train collector just like I am.

Me and my very good friend Kayle Lovell standing in front of the camera at my grad party. I will never forget all of the good times we had in Psychology class!

Me and good friend DJ April Conley smiling for the camera. I love going down to the local bar, seeing her smiling face, and singing my heart out!

Me and one of my favorite longtime friends, Brent Murphy, who I have known since third grade.

Me and my good friends Jason Light and Daniel Stepansky.

Me and another "bestie" Krystal Cella; I have known
her since third grade.

Me and my favorite neighbor Mike Henschel; I have known him my entire life, and always thought of him as a great father figure.

Me and my kindergarten teacher's daughter Jordyn Hronec having a blast at Senior Prom.

Me and my good, good, friend Paige Ellenberger; I have known her for a long time (her family, too, especially cousins Jen Sargent and daughter Cristina).

Me and my friend Braunlyn Sistek smiling for the camera at high school graduation back in June 2016.

Me and one of my favorite music teachers, Mr. Karl Faulk, who came to surprise me for a quick visit during the fall of 2021.

Me and my friend Kaylee Holtzman partying it up in the limo at Junior Prom back in 2015.

Me and one of my favorite principals, Mr. Mark Jeney, posing for the camera at Junior Prom. My favorite part of the year was hearing his Christmas phrase, "For anyone who misbehaves or acts up will get a little fa la la, rum pum pum pum, ho ho ho, and last but not least, up Versailles (Avenue) you go!"

Me and my great friend Jimmy Young standing in front of the camera after the Christmas service at Bridge City Church.

Me and a few more of my favorite teachers Mrs. Karen Bisi, Mrs. Andrea Abrams, and Mrs. Kathleen Smedley who sadly died in September of 2016.

Me and my friend Christian Harris celebrated my birthday and posed in front of the camera before I left the Roadhouse!

Here I am with Jeremy Kiger, his girlfriend Morgan Swasey, and a couple of their friends at Plaza Azteca, a Mexican restaurant not too far from my house, enjoying a late celebration for my birthday.

Here I am at Brand Name Glass with some of the guys. Standing here with me are Joe Driscoll, Nate Haight, and Nate Guzewicz.

Me and my dear friend Melanie Mills posed in front of the camera after I won the raffle at Brand Name Glass.

Me and my good friend and favorite artist Chris Beech (also known as Beechwood) posed in front of the camera at one of their shows called "April With Some Fools."

Me and my church group members went out to eat at
Primanti Brother's and watched a Pittsburgh Penguins
Game. Here with me are Jim Armstrong, Paul Yester,
Christian Larson, Bob Weakland, Tom Mazur, John
Kwiecinski, and Terry Graham.

Me and my best friend Jazzlyn George posing for the camera at my house after I gave her the bracelet I made for her.

Me and my friend Caleb Shively went out to buy some music equipment for me and then went out to grab lunch at Condado Tacos in the Downtown Section of Pittsburgh.

Me and my really close friend Alicia Howard enjoying a good ole fashioned Italian dinner at Tillie's Restaurant down in McKeesport just a few days before Memorial Day 2022.

Me and my friend Jayvawn Battle holding the chords tight for the camera after our 2016 NHS ceremony.

Me and one of my favorite guidance counselors, Mr. Lepsch, posed in front of the camera for the NHS ceremony in 2016.

Me and good friend Chandler Benjamin smiled for the camera at the 2016 NHS ceremony.

Me and my friend Hayley Kukulka posing for the camera; again, after our NHS ceremony of 2016.

Me and my great friends from NHS, Anthony Fonzi and his girlfriend, Sarah Karabinos, all smiling for the camera.

Me and my favorite neighbor Jonnie Henschel; he helped me feel better on my 16th birthday when I was having a rough moment!

Here I am down at Lake Emilie at Renzie Park on my first day of fishing in 2022. I did not catch anything the first day, but the second time I caught a nice trout and almost had two.

Me and my friend Marrla Hall taking a selfie right before getting on the bus; this was taken many years ago.

Me, my mom Catherine, and my grandma Betty, all eating out at Joe's Crab Shack down at Station Square in Pittsburgh. I believe this photo was taken during my high school years.

Me and best friend Hillary Whatley taking a selfie in
World History class back in my Junior Year.

Me dancing with my neighbor Ruth Brown at her wedding at Westwood Bar and Grill and Golf Course back in September of 2015.

Here's me at my graduation with my longtime dear friend Michael Permigiani, with his lovely mother, Tina.

And now, a few final photos! Here's me with (most of) my instrument collection. I play acoustic, bass, and electric guitar, bongos, clarinet, keyboard, and – my latest discovery – the didgeridoo. I love learning new songs in all types of genres.

As I mentioned earlier, I have discovered a love of crafting! I enjoy painting canvases, making holiday decor, and making beaded bracelets. You can see me in this photo standing next to my board of many creations in my crafting area of the basement.

Cooking is most definitely a favorite pastime. Last year, I whipped up Thanksgiving and Christmas dinners, as well as made all the New Year's Eve snacks. This year, I provided the spreads for Easter, Mother's Day, and Memorial Day. Grandma appreciates the chance to rest – and my mom admittedly can't boil water!

Made in the USA
Columbia, SC
05 March 2023

13378341R00065